YOUR KNOWLEDGE HAS VALUE

The representation of gender in the novel "Things Fall Apart" by Chinua Achebe

Nicole Piontek

Bibliographic information published by the German National Library:

The German National Library lists this publication in the National Bibliography; detailed bibliographic data are available on the Internet at http://dnb.dnb.de.

ISBN: 9783346577832
This book is also available as an ebook.

© GRIN Publishing GmbH
Nymphenburger Straße 86
80636 München

Print and binding: Books on Demand GmbH, Norderstedt, Germany
Printed on acid-free paper from responsible sources.

The present work has been carefully prepared. Nevertheless, authors and publishers do not incur liability for the correctness of information, notes, links and advice as well as any printing errors.

GRIN web shop: https://www.grin.com/document/1168357

Rheinische Friedrich-Wilhelms-Universität Bonn

Institut für Anglistik, Amerikanistik und Keltologie

The representation of gender in Achebe's *Things Fall Apart*.

Term paper for

Postcolonial Literatures and Cultures

Winter Term 2020/21

Nicole Piontek

Table of Contents

1. Introduction

This paper is going to argue whether Achebe's novel *Things Fall Apart* illustrates an Ibo society with socially constructed gender roles. Male dominance and supremacy are visible throughout the whole novel, just as the subordination and discrimination of the female gender. Moreover, the novel depicts numerous gender stereotypes, which will be analysed in this paper to achieve a better understanding of the gender ideologies in Achebe's society. Strong gender roles can be seen in various situations in the life of Okonkwo, which is why this paper is going to be focussed on different aspects in the life of the protagonist of the novel. Beside the question whether *Things Fall Apart* portrays strong masculine dominance, the following questions will be answered: Are there differences in the various spaces regarding gender roles in the novel? Is there an aspect in Ibo's society in which the subordination of women is broken? These questions allow the paper to take female rebellion into consideration and to keep the analysis open to a variety of readings of the novel without purely focussing on the reader's first impression of the dominance of manhood.

Firstly, this paper is going to explain key terms and concepts which one needs while talking about gender. Here, the difference between *gender* and *sex* is explained, just as various concepts of sexism and subordination of women in text and language. Although Achebe's work is written in 1959, this chapter will explain the state of the art, as the following analysis is going to consider gender roles in Achebe's novel from today's perspective. Secondly, a description of gender roles in the traditional Ibo society is going to follow. This will help to put Achebe's work into context and to increase the analysis of Achebe's authenticity and credibility.

The analysis of *Things Fall Apart* is structured into four aspects, which are all embracing the protagonist's life. Firstly, a comparison of Okonkwo and his father is going to offer an introduction to Okonkwo's character as well as a comparison of two different male characters. As Okonkwo and his father stand in contrast to each other this chapter is going to analyse in how far this contrast is affecting the portrayal of the male gender in the society as a whole. The chapter on 'Family and Property' is going to analyse Okonkwo's private life and the role of men and women in families. Thirdly, gender roles in public life will be discussed. Achebe writes about numerous social gatherings. In how far these portray the dominance of manhood is going to be analysed in this chapter. Finally, the analysis is going to focus on religion and the divine and the questions whether the depiction of gender roles in the Ibo's belief system correlates with the one in public life.

2. Exploration of Gender Roles

2.1. *Conceptualizing Gender*

Although the history of gender is relatively short, there do exist certain key words and concepts which are of importance while talking about gender roles. Some of them will be described in the following. First, one must acknowledge the difference between *sex* and *gender*. On the one hand, *sex* refers to the "biological state of being female or male." (Sauntson 2) This term is not only used for humans, but also for animals (cf. ibid.). *Gender* on the other hand only describes human beings. Gender is constructed through "a social categorisation system consisting of a polarised set of behaviours classed as 'masculine' and 'feminine'." (ibid.) Therefore, *gender* is linked to *sex* to some extent, as the different sets of behaviours are assigned to the biological states (cf. ibid). While talking about the correlation of *gender* and *sex* the terms *cisgendered* and *transgendered* are of importance. *Cisgendered* is a person "whose chosen gender identity corresponds to their biological sex." (ibid.), whereas *transgendered* describes a person who does not identify with their biological sex.

Moreover, Sauntson argues that "Gender is seen as an organising principle for social life in that behavioural expectations around masculinity and femininity are set up through the repetition of social norms." (Sauntson 3) According to Sauntson, gender organises and structures society and with it appears a kind of hierarchy between gender. Especially in the past, men were considered the dominant gender (cf. ibid.). These expectations of the two different gender can be summarized with the term *Gender Ideology*.

As gender ideologies are shaped by society, also the subordinate gender plays along, as these "ideologies are not upheld or perpetuated in society by force, rather they become naturalised so that people consent or 'sign up to' ideologies without really questioning them." (Sauntson 10). According to Sauntson the subordinate gender naturally loses agency by playing along with the dominant gender. Furthermore, gender ideologies and hierarchies are strengthened by commonly accepted gender stereotypes.

Gender stereotypes are differences between men and women that are being exaggerated and overgeneralized, which leads to an overall distorted perception of gender, such as "[…] tools being for boys and jewellery being for girls […]." (ibid.)

2

Gender stereotypes can be divided into: "four distinct components of gender: traits, role behaviours, physical characteristics, and occupations" (Haines 354). Stereotypical male traits are for instance: braveness, competitiveness, and a higher tendency towards violence. In contrast, female traits are more sensitive and emotional. This is again picked up in physical characteristics, as stereotypical men have a strong anatomy, short hair and a tough appearance and stereotypical women have a soft body, long hair, and a more elegant appearance. When it comes to role behaviours and occupations, a stereotypical man is more educated and works in higher occupations, whereas a stereotypical woman stays at home with housework and the upbringing of their children (cf. ibid. 353 f.).

Additionally, gender stereotyping does not only lead to a distorted perception, but it "may, for example, limit the expression of individuals' aptitudes and interests." (Liben 2) This is already visible in preschool children's behaviour, as they automatically separate in same-sex groups (cf. Maccoby 55). Furthermore, such a behaviour can limit or even shape children's development, as Liben argues: "Even theorists who disagree about the relative role of cognitive versus environmental factors agree that children's assimilation of cultural stereotypes plays a role in guiding and shaping their own gender role behavior." (Liben 14). For instance, when a boy is confronted with a doll, it is likely that he refuses to play with it because of socially constructed gender stereotypes (cf. ibid.). But also "[c]hallenging gender stereotypes" (Mulvey 681) is difficult, as it "can also lead to social isolation" (ibid.), which shows that already children are dependent on the constructed gender roles to live a life in society. Hence, gender stereotypes lead to a cognitive gap between women and men, which then leads to abuse of power as the stereotypical man is stronger and more powerful than the stereotypical woman. Thus, gender ideologies and gender roles with a hierarchy are created. Analysing how these gender ideologies are represented in texts is a useful approach in gender studies (cf. Sauntson 1).

There are different approaches to deal with gender roles in texts. Part of them is focussing on "'minoritised' genders and sexualities such as lesbian, gay, bisexual, transgender plus (LGBT+) identities." (ibid.) But also a focus on "more 'hegemonic' identities, such as heterosexuality and hegemonic masculinity" (ibid.) is a reasonable approach. Especially with the previously mentioned strong gender ideologies constructed by society, there do still exist patriarchal societies and "we would expect there to be many representations which serve to potentially disempower (some) women and girls." (ibid. 6) One way of pointing out the dominant gender is by demonstrating sexism in language:

"'sexist language' has come to be defined as language which is used in ways which ignore, define and degrade women." (Sauntson 145)

Sexist language can be divided into direct- and indirect sexist language. Direct sexist language "[…] refers to any use of language which makes an explicit or implicit assumption that the 'male' or 'masculine' is either the norm or is representative of all human beings." (ibid. 146), this is mostly visible by using generic masculine forms such as masculine pronouns, nouns, adjectives and "any other linguistic forms which present 'man' as representative of 'humans/people'." (ibid.) Therefore, everytime language is used to state that men are the dominant gender and women are subordinate can be regarded sexist language. But also omitting feminine expressions is excluding women and thus subjugating their gender. There are many more ways of sexist language, for instance semantic derogation, which means words that originally were neutral become negative or even insulting throughout time i.e., spinster or mistress (cf. ibid. 147). Indirect sexism can be seen in different ways. One is sexist humour, which Sauntson describes as follows: "Humour […] often exaggerates certain features associated with a group or draws on and plays with stereotypical knowledge for comic effect." (ibid. 150) This happens for instance, when a woman says things which have the opposite meaning: Yes = No; We need = I want; We need to talk = I need to complain (cf. ibid.)[1]. Another way of indirect sexism are presuppositions. For instance, "'So, have you women finished gossiping?'" (ibid. 152), this automatically links gossiping to the feminine gender. Additionally, silence is a way of indirect sexist language, as sexism can be achieved "through what is *not* said/written" (ibid. 158). All in all, while talking about gender there are many concepts and approaches which must be taken into consideration. The approaches now mentioned will be used in the discussion of Achebe's *Things Fall Apart*.

2.2.   Gender in the traditional Ibo society

This chapter is going to give a theoretical overview of gender roles in the traditional Ibo society. Most studies that deal with gender in the traditional Ibo society lead to the description of masculine and feminine cisgendered people. This is already visible in the naming of Ibo people. Onukawa argues in her study: "Our sampling shows that gender-specific names constitute more than 90 per cent of Igbo names. […] Only a tiny percentage of Igbo names (less than 10 per cent) are gender-neutral, borne by both males and females." (Onukawa 108) The author's sampling of Ibo names shows that there is a

---

[1] For the full table of Women's and Men's language translated see Sauntson 150 f.

clear distinction between men and women in the Ibo culture. Furthermore, there is also a difference in the dominance of gender.

The dominance of manhood in the traditional Ibo culture is visible in family life. Ibo families usually have a masculine leader, who "is often seen as the 'president', the king, the administrator of his umunna family." (Iloanusi 113) Hence, wives have a subordinate role in families. Additionally, according to Iloanusi, men are expected to have strong families with sons, which is why monogamous families are not the norm in Ibo cultures to ensure the birth of male children (cf. ibid.). Moreover, the precolonial political situation in the Ibo culture further strengthens the dominance of manhood.

Even though political power is wielded by both men and women, there are differences in their extent (cf. Chuku 82). Generally, the political situation is decentralized, which means that there is not one political system but many different variations throughout the regions. This leads to a "wide dispersal of political authority among the sexes, age grades, secret and title societies, and such religious practitioners as diviners, priests, and priestesses." (ibid. 83) that makes it difficult to distinguish one specific authority. Nevertheless, Chuku uses two models of political systems to highlight gender specific aspects in the political situation. The first model is a cooperate political system which is dominated by men but gives women restricted opportunities to be politicly active: "women become political actors based on their kinship relationships as daughters, sisters, mothers, wives, and in-laws to men." (ibid.) Chuku continues:

> In the case of the Igbo, authority was in the hands of the eze or obi (king) and ndichie (all-male council of elders and title holders). [...] Certain women in these polities wielded important political power and authority as well. Such women included the hi Ada (oldest daughter of the lineage), royal women, and heads of women's organizations. (ibid.)

Although women have positions and authorities in this political system, these are linked to their relations with men which makes them subordinate to manhood.

The second model is a dual-sex political system where men and women each have their own political structures (cf. ibid. 84). This way "Women exercised direct political power within arenas viewed as the female province through all female organizations. Such female organizations included women's courts, market authorities, secret societies, and age-grade institutions." (ibid.) Here, women are not bound to their relations with men but still are secluded from the political structures of men. Additionally, religion in the traditional Ibo cultures highlights these gender ideologies once more.

Again, both genders are included in the religious setting. However, the dominance of manhood becomes clear very quickly: "It is interesting that male domination of social reality is reflected at the religious level by the fact that Chineke/Chukwu/Obasi and his powerful manifestations or agents [...] are all male gods." (Kalu 186) and adding to that also their priests are male. Nevertheless, in the living world the practices of religion become more complex regarding gender ideologies. There do exist female deities and it even has been argued that the goddess *Ala* was once the supreme deity (cf. ibid. 187). Although female deities exist, their priests are always male and thus have control over them by overseeing shrines, sacrifices and other rituals (cf. 188). Therefore, the dominance of manhood is repeatedly breaking any attempt of female authority may it be in family- or public life.

3. Gender in Achebe's *Things Fall Apart*

3.1.   Okonkwo and his father in comparison

Achebe's novel begins with an introduction of the two characters Okonkwo and his father Unoka which offers a contrast of two different types of men. The distinction of these characters and the resulting characteristics of masculinity will be analysed in this chapter. In the beginning of the first chapter, Okonkwo is represented as a famous man who achieved success through masculine acts and violence. Quickly the topic of fighting and violence is introduced. Okonkwo "had brought honor to his village" (Achebe 3) by winning a difficult wrestling game at a young age. It is clear that "From a very early age, Okonkwo is obsessed with championing his masculinity [...]." (Osei-Nyame 151) Additionally, the fight does not only show Okonkwo's disposition for fighting but it also introduces the dominance of manhood as the protagonist won against a fighter called "Amalinze the Cat" (ibid.). Here, Alsyouf argues that "the name "Cat" is not incidental; it is a clear symbol of femininity. The fighting scene therefore is an implication of Okonkwo's early and serious attempts to subordinate femininity in the novel's world." (Alsyouf 175) Thus, Achebe creates a stereotypical strong masculine character and foreshadows the dominance of manhood already in the first paragraph of the novel. This description of strength and violence continues as Okonkwo is described being "tall and huge, and his bushy eyebrows and wide nose gave him a very severe look." (Achebe 3f.) Furthermore, it is said that "he did pounce on people quite often." (ibid. 4) what again highlights his violent behaviour. Hereafter, Unoka is introduced who stands in strong contrast to Okonkwo.

Unoka is linked to more sensitive characteristics and less violence. Simultaneously, he is depicted as being unsuccessful. His lack of success is the first thing the reader learns about Okonkwo's father: "He [Okonkwo] had no patience with

6

unsuccessful men. He had no patience with his father." (ibid.) This anaphor highlights the connection of being unsuccessful and his father. Furthermore, Unoka was a "deptor" (ibid.) who had depts everywhere, and he was "tall but very thin and had a slight stoop. He wore a haggard and mournful look [...]." (ibid.) Hence, even his physical appearance represents failure and not strength, just like his interests: He had a passion for music which always gave him peace and he loved kites, children and sitting around warm fires (cf. ibid. 3f.). The description of his passion is quickly interrupted with the words: "Unoka, the grown-up, was a failure." (ibid. 5) The passion for music and his other sensible interests do not lead to success and money because of his lack of strength. This is shown through the conversation with Okoye.

Okoye was a musician himself, but he was also interested in talking about wars, opposed to Unoka who "was never happy when it came to wars. He is in fact a coward and could not bear the sight of blood." (ibid. 6) This again creates a connection of violence and success, as Okoye was "not a failure like Unoka" (ibid.) and had "a large barne full of yams and he had three wives. And now he was going to take the Idemili title, the third highest in the land." (ibid.) Here, one does learn more attributes that belong to a successful man: property, multiple wives, and titles; all of which Unoka does not have. The conversation further strengthens the seriousness of Unoka's depts, as Unoka does not want to pay back Okoye. Osei-Nyame argues: "Negotiating his survival while trapped by economic necessity, Unoka, pelled into being resourceful, is also at his most articulate." (Osei-Nyame 153) It is said that language is regarded as particularly important in the Ibo culture (cf. Achebe 7). According to Osei-Nyame, Unoka made use of this custom as "Unoka's response is most significant for its manipulation of the wisdom implicit in the language of proverbs as a strategy of survival by deferring the debt he owes." (ibid.) This shows that Unoka acknowledged the Ibo society and with it the concept of masculine success. Nevertheless, Unoka only used the knowledge to secure his survival without actually improving his situation.

This way he stayed poor and without a title, thus unsuccessful, until he died (cf. ibid 8). Scheub summarizes the description of Unoka as follows: "This, then, was Okonkwo's father: a lover of beauty and a connoisseur of joy, well acquainted with sorrow and the scorn of his fellows." (Scheub 111) This description highlights Unoka's sensible character which ultimately led him to failure. Still, his failure does not affect his son on every level.

At the end of the first chapter the connection of Okonkwo and his father is stated to be primarily on a psychological level. Okonkwo was ashamed of his father (cf. Achebe

8), but he is not limited by his father's faults: "Fortunately, among these people a man was judged according to his worth and not according to the worth of his father." (ibid.) Consequently, Okonkwo did not carry his father's depts. And thus, his success is again highlighted:

> He was still young but he had won fame as the greatest wrestler in the nine villages. He was a wealthy farmer and had two barns full of yams, and had just married his third wife. To crown it all he had taken two titles and had shown incredible prowess in two inter-tribal wars. (ibid.)

This description of his success is strengthened as it is written right after the description of Unoka's failure. "Throughout, Achebe emphasizes Okonkwo's bravery and fearlessness; he is the complete antithesis to his weak father, Unoka." (Jua 200) This antithesis strengthens the depiction and importance of success. Because of that, Okonkwo's hard work is based on the fear of becoming as unsuccessful as his father. This is repeatedly mentioned in the novel, i.e.: "He was a man of action, a man of war. Unlike his father he could stand the look of blood." (Achebe 10) and "It was the fear of himself, lest he should be found to resemble his father." (ibid. 13) Furthermore, Scheub states: "Through hard work, Okonkwo would be able to accomplish two things: he would exorcise, to some extent at least, the spirit of his father, and he would simultaneously gain the approbation of his peers." (Scheub 112) If Okonkwo achieves an exorcism of his father's spirit, he would be psychologically free, but this would not change his material situation, which shows that his fear is set on a psychological level. This also demonstrates that men in Achebe's Ibo society are under pressure to achieve success. Therefore, the description of these two different characters in the beginning of the novel creates a depiction of a society where men are linked to hard work, violence, and responsibility. Thus, men are represented as the dominant gender as these aspects do not apply to women. Besides, the concept of gender ideologies is introduced and along with these come socially constructed gender roles and typical gender stereotypes, which are all signs of the discrimination of the female sex. This happens throughout the whole novel, as the following chapters will demonstrate.

3.2.   Family and Property

The dominance of manhood is further strengthened with the description of Okonkwo's family and property. This chapter analyses various aspects of the private life of the protagonist in the context of gender roles. As it comes to property, it generally belongs to men in Achebe's Ibo culture. Linked to Unoka's missing success is the fact that Okonkwo did not inherit any property: "With a father like Unoka, Okonkwo did not have the start in life which many young men had. He neither inherited a barn nor a title, nor even a young wife." (Achebe 18) Not only does this show how property is inherited from father to son, but what is considered as property.

Here, women are considered property which subordinates women in every aspect. This depiction is strengthened again with the description of Nwakibie's household: "There was a wealthy man in Okonkwo's village who had three huge barns, nine wives and thirty children." (ibid. 18) Consequently, more women equal more property. Moreover, Okonkwo gains success and property: "He had a large barn full of yams and he has three wives." (ibid. 5) Ijem argues that the possibility of increasing his property comes with his masculinity:

> Okonkwo's wealth points to his industriousness which the masculine gender is known for in Achebe's *Things Fall Apart*, while his masculinity enables him to marry three wives and keep them under his control. Thus the male and female genders have been unevenly portrayed. (Ijem 57)

Furthermore, property needs care and control, which means that men need to control their wives. Achebe writes: "No matter how prosperous a man was, if he was unable to rule his women and his children (and especially his women) he was not really a man." (Achebe 53) Overall, the subordination of women becomes obvious while talking about property. But there are more aspects that highlight the separation of manhood and the womenfolk.

The womenfolk have their own hierarchy and rules in the society. Anasi, the oldest of Nwakibie's wives, is described as follows:

> Anasi was a middle-aged woman, tall and strongly built. There was authority in her bearing and she looked every inch the ruler of the womenfolk in a large and prosperous family. She wore the anklet of her husband's title, which the first wife alone could wear. (ibid. 20)

She is described as a ruler, but seclusively in her family. Her agency is limited to her family. Furthermore, she wears her husband's title and is thus defined by him. Therefore, women take part in society but only limited as wives and mothers. There is hardly a description of a woman out of a family situation in Achebe's novel. Moreover, marriage is a man's matter as well.

Women are traded into marriage by their male family members. This can be seen in the scene in which the visit of the suitor of Obierika's daughter Akueke "turns to a commercial bargain." (Alsyouf 176) During the negotiation of the bride-price Akueke is not present. She only enters one time to present herself and to be looked at (cf. Achebe 71). The negotiation then "turns to a bargain […]." (Alsyouf 176) in which the men act traders "exposing cheap goods to sell." (ibid.) After the bargain is finished the women join the company by serving food (cf. Achebe 73). The women's role is limited to serving and pleasuring men, they do not have any agency when it comes to decisions regarding their own lives. Alsyouf further argues: "This scene is crucial in solidifying the powers of hegemonic masculinity." (Alsyouf 176) Alsyouf statement can be underlined with the following quote: "but even if you came into your obi and found her lover on top of her, you would still have committed a great evil to beat her [during the week of peace]." (Achebe 30) This quote shows that women are not allowed to have multiple men on their side, whereas men become more prosperous having multiple women. Thus, marriage is an example of how men control women and separate themselves from the other gender. Moreover, with marriage come children and again masculinity is represented dominantly.

Childbirth is the most important aspect in the life of an Ibo woman in Achebe's novel: "The birth of her children, which should be a woman's crowning glory [...]" (ibid. 77). Still, there are differences whether a girl or a boy is born. Okonkwo's behaviour towards Ezinma highlights the fact of sons being superior. He repeatedly states that he likes his daughter but regrets her being a girl: "He never stopped regretting that Ezinma was a girl. Of all his children she alone understood his every mood." (ibid. 172) Throughout the novel this might be the noblest compliment of Okonkwo and this one "he gives to his beloved daughter Ezinma." (Scheub 113) This strengthens Okonkwo's love for his daughter, but also highlights his suffering of her being born female. Moreover, women are not only defined by their husbands but also by their sons. The reader never learns the name of Okonkwo's only wife who has a son. She is always called "Nwoye's mother" (i.e., Achebe 27), whereas all his other wives, who only have daughters, are named (Ekwefi and Ojiugo). Therefore, women live to bear children and are defined by their husbands and sons. Additionally, the different sets of emotions are emphasized with the upbringing of children.

Ekwefi is described as a loving mother. In contrast, Okonkwo cares for his children, especially Ezinma, but does not show his emotions openly. For him, showing emotions openly is a weakness (cf. ibid. 28). When Ikemefuna is killed and his son Nwoye overhears what had happened, he "bursts into tears." (ibid. 57) and is immediately judged by his father as crying is a sign of weakness (cf. ibid). Shortly after follows his wife's reaction. She hugs her son and shows affection (cf. ibid. 58). This points out the different behaviours of men and women. Furthermore, Okonkwo suffers because of the death of Ikemefuna and calls himself a woman due to his emotions. Ijem states: "This implies that weakness and fear are associated with women and not men." (Ijem 59) as men are supposed to be strong and superior. Moreover, the whole act of killing Ikemefuna antagonizes the earth goddess Ani and sets "in motion a chain of events which ultimately leads to his [Okonkwo's] downfall." (Cobham 170). One can argue that Okonkwo's denial of emotions for Ikemefuna led to him killing his "adopted son" and ultimately to his suicide. Nevertheless, certain emotions are set to be for women in Achebe's novel. This is exemplified with the aspect of storytelling for children.

Both genders interact with their children and tell them stories. Still, these stories differ in content. Mothers tell creative stories which carry moral and meaning (cf. Achebe 53), whereas Okonkwo tells his son "masculine stories of violence and bloodshed." (p. 54). As fathers only tell their sons stories, only they get in touch with the topic of violence. This education leads to differences between the upbringing of girls and boys. Hence, gender is almost predestined to polarize (cf. Ijem 59). Moreover, the novel mentions Okonkwo's mother only on a few occasions. One of them is Okonkwo's memory of a story his mother once told. Although he does remember this story from his childhood he calls is "silly as all women's stories." (Achebe 75) Still, this memory emphasizes the importance of storytelling as throughout the novel his relationship with his father is foregrounded and his mother is neglected (cf. Jeyifo 849). Therefore, storytelling acts as a motive for gender indifference in the novel. Apart from this, it also highlights the predestined gender roles of Achebe's Ibo children, as the education teaches them certain behaviours which are connected to their biological sex and ultimately lead to distorted gender perceptions (cf. Maccoby 55). Moreover, the topic of violence is not only visible in storytelling but in the everyday life of the protagonist.

Okonkwo's first description was already linked to violence and disrespect towards women. This depiction continues: "Okonkwo ruled his household with a heavy hand." (Achebe 13) His wives and his children fear him because of his harsh behaviour. It is described multiple times that Okonkwo hits his family members: One time his youngest wife did not cook for him in time which is why he beats her "very heavily" (ibid. 29); another time Okonkwo beats and even shoots his wife for trivial reasons, just out of his anger (cf. ibid. 38). Alsyouf argues: "He [Okonkwo] believes that violence and oppressiveness are an expression of masculinity." (Alsyouf 175), which is why he chooses to behave this violently. In addition, his disrespect towards the feminine gender is shown through his speech as well, i.e.: "Do what you are told, woman […]" (Achebe 14) and "Sit like a woman!" (ibid. 44). Through these phrases Okonkwo is using direct sexist language and is therefore disrespectful on the one hand, and on the other hand highlights the subordination of women, just like the violence against them does. Nevertheless, there is one passage in the novel which creates a feeling of hypocrisy regarding the depiction of women.

While Uchendu talks about the concept of "Mother is Supreme" he describes two constructed genders that act accordingly to their given gender roles:

> It's true that a child belongs to its father. But when a father beats his child, it seeks sympathy in it's mother's hut. A man belongs to his fatherland when things are good and life is sweet. But when there is sorrow and bitterness he finds refuge in his motherland. Your mother is there to protect you. (ibid. 134)

He describes, as Rhoads states: "The entire Igbo society is based upon the combining of the male and female principles. The male is strong and warlike, and the female is tender and supportive in times of adversity. Uncle Uchendu explains this balance in his explication of the saying "Mother is Supreme"." (Rhoads 65) Thus, Uchendu sums up what one has learned about the Ibo society so far: the masculine gender is strong, and the feminine gender is sensitive. Still, this description does not address the imbalance of justice and rights of both genders or, as Stratton puts it, it "exposes the hypocrisy of his forebears' gender ideology." (Stratton 166) Uchendu's concept of 'Mother is Supreme' is full of gender stereotypes and sexist language. Overall, the masculine gender is evidently dominant in family life in Achebe's novel. The subordination of women is visible in every aspect when it comes to property, marriage, and children and is further strengthened in the public life of Achebe' society.

3.3. Public Life

There are multiple public gatherings in *Things Fall Apart*, all of which demonstrate gender roles in public life. In the following, a selection of these is analysed. The first gathering is about the killing of a daughter of Umuofia and illustrates the exclusion of women. As the bells of Umuofia called for the gathering it is stated that "Every man of Umuofia was asked to gather at the market place tomorrow morning." (Achebe 9) Hence, women are not invited to the happening. A daughter was killed, and all men shout in thirst for blood (cf. ibid. 10), the men want revenge and feel responsible for the lack of protection of the girl. This is a way of portraying dominance over women, as a woman is considered to not be able to look out for herself. In addition, the men demand "a young man and a virgin as compensation." (ibid. 11) Here, the woman is linked to sexuality, whereas the man is linked to age. Moreover, the reader never finds out the name of the virgin. Again, this shows discrimination of the female sex. There are two more gatherings which demonstrate the same issue.

One is the trial of Mgbafo. Here, women are present but the author highlights that this gathering is not supposed to be for their attendance: "It was clear from the way the crowd stood or sat that the ceremony was for men. There were many women, but they looked on from the fringe like outsiders." (ibid. 87) This time, the exclusion of women is directly addressed. Although the trial deals with the woman Mgbafo, she is not allowed to represent herself: "Women are to be seen and not heard. Achebe's society is a patriarchal society. Mgbafo herself who is directly involved in the matter has to be represented by her brothers since society has considered it unacceptable for a woman to talk before men." (Ijem 59) Ijem emphasizes the subordination of women in this matter. Furthermore, the trial ends by stating that "It is not bravery when a man fights a woman." (Achebe 93) The notion of women needing protection is picked up, which strengthens women's incapability of acting for their own rights. Furthermore, the burial of Ezeudu emphasizes the subordination of women once more.

The burial is attended, again, only by men (cf. ibid. 121). Additionally, the process of a man's life is described as follows:

> The land of the living was not far removed from the domain of the ancestors. There was coming and going between them, especially at festivals and also when an old man died, because an old man was very close to the ancestors. A man's life from birth to death was a series of transition rites which brought him nearer and nearer to his ancestors. (ibid. 122)

This description of dying and reuniting with one's ancestors does not include women. It is not stated whether this also happens when a woman dies, or whether this privilege is exclusively reserved for manhood. The omitting of feminine expressions excludes the feminine gender in this situation. However, there is one public occasion that stands in contrast to the others, at least at first glance.

The gathering for the wrestling match includes both men and women. Still, it shows discrimination of the feminine gender on a different level. The scene begins by stating that the following happening is for everyone: "The whole village turned out on the *ilo*, men, women and children." (ibid. 46) Nevertheless, women are only allowed to watch and are not allowed to participate in a wrestling match themselves: "While the men wrestle, the women as passive creatures could only watch, clap and laugh." (Ijem 58) All wrestlers in Achebe's novel are men (cf. Achebe 47). The act of wrestling is described as a mixture of technique and strength (cf. ibid.), and women are not capable of these skills. Ijem emphasizes this depiction by stating: "Wrestling requires a lot of energy and tact which only the men, as the stronger and superior beings possess." (Ijem 58) Although this scene allows women to be part of the public gathering, it still excludes them from participating fully. Women are passive and subordinate in this scene, just like in the gatherings described before. In addition, the scene in which Okonkwo shoots a member further emphasizes the dominance of manhood.

This scene demonstrates how women are discriminated indirectly. Crimes in Achebe's Ibo society can be male or female, as one can see with the description of Okonkwo's shooting: "The crime was of two kinds, male and female." (Achebe 124) The differentiation of a male and a female crime emphasizes the separation of the gender. Achebe continues: "Okonkwo had committed the female, because it was inadvertent." (ibid.) The female sex is considered the weaker sex and is therefore not capable of committing a serious crime, which is why a crime that happened inadvertently is called a female crime. Later Uchendu calls Okonkwo's crime: "It is a female *ochu*." (ibid. 129) Here, the existence of male and female crimes is emphasized ones more. However, the shooting scene offers yet another viewpoint and a contrast to the character Okonkwo.

His friend Obierika shares different values and can be weighed as Okonkwo's counterpart. While Okonkwo is "a flat character embodying the best in the Ibo culture's notion of manliness and masculinity [...]." (Anyokwu 19) Obierika represents a more balanced view. As Cobham argues: "Okonkwo's limited personal understanding of physical ascendancy and his equation of courage with masculinity are set against a much richer and more complex set of values available to his clan as a whole." (Cobham 170) Generally, Obierika can be considered "the main spokesman for this greater tradition" (ibid.). His words repeatedly stand in contrast to Okonkwo's action and allow a hint at a more complex society (cf. ibid). This is visible in the shooting scene as well. Obierika questions Okonkwo's exile: "Why should a man suffer so grievously for an offense he had committed inadvertently?" (Achebe 125) Still, he helps to destroy Okonkwo's farm, even though he does not understand the reasons for this punishment. In summary, public life in Achebe's novel clearly demonstrates the dominance of manhood and the subordination and discrimination of women. The society is bound to strong gender ideologies that lead to direct and indirect gender discrimination throughout the whole public sphere and even beyond, as will be analysed in the following chapter.

3.4. Religion and the divine

Religion is omnipresent in *Things Fall Apart*. Especially the description of goddesses is foregrounded in the novel, which is why this chapter will focus on the female deities. Like in the traditional Ibo society, in Achebe's culture some female deities have male priests and are controlled by the male public. For instance, the earth goddess Ani, who "played a greater part in the life of the people than any other deity. She was the ultimate judge of communion with the departed fathers of the clan whose bodies had been committed to earth." (Achebe 29) In addition to this Scheub calls Ani: "a major figure in the Umuofian pantheon and a central pillar of social traditions [...]." (Scheub 103) Despite her important role and her high regard, she is controlled by a male priest: "Ezeani, the priest of the earth goddess." (Achebe 29) Hence, the ultimate power lies in the hand of the masculine gender, as Ezeani is the one who performs rituals and punishments (cf. ibid.). In contrast to Ani stands Agbala, the Oracle of the Hills and the Caves.

While Ani is undermined by the existence of a male priest, Agbala is empowered by her priestess and vice versa. The reader learns about two priestesses in the novel. The first one is Chika, whom Unoka encounters. She is depicted as a "dark figure" (ibid. 17) who is "full of power of her god, and she was greatly feared." (ibid.) Men respected the goddess Agbala, as well as her priestess. Here, women gain power and for the first time are not subordinate to the manhood. Chika is evidently considered a powerful woman, just like the later priestess Chielo.

The power of the woman Chielo is emphasized with her visit of Okonkwo and his family to pick up Ezinma. It is the only time in the novel, where Okonkwo is forced to follow the orders of a woman. Still, he does this reluctantly: "Okonkwo pleaded with her to come back in the morning because Ezinma was now asleep." (ibid. 100) Nevertheless, Chielo is superior in this instance and takes his daughter with her. Ezinma's mother, Ekwefi, follows the priestess while Okonkwo stays behind as they are not allowed to follow Chielo. Osei-Nyame argues that this scene breaks the socially constructed gender roles in the novel to some point:

> Bearing in mind the sexual difference and gendered politics of the novel that are articulated especially within the overt masculinist ideological framework that contextualizes the assertions of Okonkwo and the patriarchs of Umuofian society, we must look beyond the surface interpretation of the episode as journey and attempt a theoretical reflection that extends the surface meaning of the Chielo-Ezinma-Ekwefi encounter to locate it as an alternative Igbo nationalist tradition within which we can construct a specifically female-centered paradigm of resistance. (Osei-Nyame 157)

According to Osei-Nyame, Ezinma and Chielo demonstrate power in this scene. Alsyouf emphasizes this argumentation by stating that the scene "demonstrates the feminine qualities repressed by powers of hegemonic masculinity; qualities that women can employ in times of distress and dangers for the good of the family and the society." (Alsyouf 178) Therefore, the women in this scene show power as well as rebellion towards the constructed gender roles in the society. However, this power is undermined, as Achebe writes: "How a woman could carry a child of that size so easily and for so long was a miracle. But Ekwefi was not thinking about that. Chielo was not a woman that night." (Achebe 107) Here, the author tries to take away the notion of feminine power and explains it with the divine. Scheub argues: "Chielo, a good a generous neighbor, becomes a fearful person when she assumes the role of Agbala's priestess […]." (Scheub 102) Therefore, Chielo becomes a different person while being a priestess. Hence, it may be argued that this scene is more about becoming divine than being of female sex. In addition, women are considered weak in the context of religion.

When Nwoye goes to the evangelists, women are discriminated once more through indirect sexist language and gender stereotyping. Okonkwo asks himself: "How could he have begotten a woman for a son?" (Achebe 153) when he learns about Nwoye turning to the protestants. Here, Ijem argues that as men are the stronger sex, they could not show such a weakness as to turn to Christian faith (cf. Ijem 60). This weakness is linked to being a woman, which is why he thinks of his son as a woman. To conclude, Achebe hints at female power when it comes to religion and the divine. However, male supremacy and the weakness of women is still foregrounded, as there are still more powerful male deities such as Chukwu (cf. Achebe 180) and the egwugwu (cf. ibid. 186). Overall, there is a definite dominance of manhood demonstrated throughout the whole novel. There is little agency for women, and whenever there seems to appear some, it is quickly undermined by the male public.

4. Conclusion

In conclusion, this paper demonstrates that there is indeed a strong dominance of the masculine gender in Achebe's *Things Fall Apart*. First and foremost, Achebe does not differentiate between *sex* and *gender*. Therefore, in his depiction of the Ibo society there do only exist cisgendered people, every female born person is considered a woman and vice versa. Hence, gender roles are limited to the biological sexes being female and male. Moreover, gender ideologies and gender stereotypes are omnipresent throughout the whole plot, and these are linked to sexist language, both direct and indirect. Altogether, the novel demonstrates a patriarchal system which is led by heterosexual, hegemonic masculinity.

The protagonist's discrimination of women is described in vivid detail throughout all spaces of Ibo's life. Firstly, the contrast between the protagonist and his father offers an introduction to masculine character trades which are mainly strength, violence, and power. As it comes to the private life in families this characterisation continues. Okonkwo is violent towards his wives and children. Furthermore, women live in separate *huts* and are treated as property rather than individual human beings with equal rights. Generally, property belongs to men and even marriage is a male process in which the masculine members of a family make decisions about the women's destiny. These constructed gender roles are part of children's education and upbringing. Sons are considered more valuable and have more connection to their fathers than daughters. The same concepts can be seen in public life, where women are actively excluded from official and social gatherings and are at most allowed as spectators, such as during the wrestling and the trial of Mgbafo. In addition, the representation of gender in religion might hint at agency for women as there do exist female deities and priestesses. Still, this could also be explained with the ultimate power of the divine. For a clear result, this must be analysed in more detail in the future.

Overall, this paper evidently describes the dominance and supremacy of manhood in Achebe's *Things Fall Apart*. The novel includes strong gender roles in which women are the subordinate gender with little agency and no rebellion. Achebe's depiction of an Ibo society correlates with the traditional precolonial Ibo society in most parts. Though, his protagonist Okonkwo is depicted as extremely violent and disrespectful towards women on a level which cannot be found in the traditional Ibo culture. To conclude, Achebe created a society with strong socially constructed gender roles in which the female sex is systematically subordinated, discriminated, and disrespected.

5. Bibliography

Primary Literature

Achebe, Chinua. *Things Fall Apart.* Penguin Books, 2017.

Secondary Literature

Alsyouf, Amjad. "Hegemonic Masculinity in Archetypal African Novels." *INFORMASI: Kajian Ilmu Komunikasi,* vol. 48, no. 2, 2018, pp. 169-179.

Anyokwu, Christopher. "Re-Imagining Gender in Chinua Achebe's "Things Fall Apart"." *Interdisciplinary Literary Studies,* vol. 12, no. 2, Spring 2011, pp. 16-31.

Chuku, Gloria. "Igbo Women and Political Participation in Nigeria, 1800s – 2005." *The International Journal of African Historical Studies,* vol. 42, no. 1, 2009, pp. 81-103.

Cobham, Rhonda. "Problems of Gender and History in the Teaching of *Things Fall Apart.*" *Chinua Achebe's Things Fall Apart. A Casebook,* edited by Isidore Okpewho. Oxford University Press, 2003, pp. 165-180.

Haines, Elizabeth L., et al. "The Times They Are A-Changing … or Are They Not? A Comparison of Gender Stereotypes, 1983–2014." *Psychology of Women Quarterly,* vol. 40, no. 3, Sept. 2016, pp. 353–363.

Ijem, Blessing U. and Isaiah I. Agbo. "Language and Gender Representation in Chinua Achebe's *Things Fall Apart.*" *English Language Teaching,* vol. 12, no. 11, Oct. 2019, pp. 55-63.

Iloanusi, Obiakoizu A. *Myths of the Creation of Man and the Origin of Death in Africa.* Peter Lang GmbH, 1984.

Jeyifo, Biodun. "Okonkwo and His Mother: Things Fall Apart and Issues of Gender in the Constitution of African Postcolonial Discourse." *Callaloo,* vol. 16, no. 4, Autumn 1993, pp. 847-858.

Jua, Roselyne M. "*Things Fall Apart* and Achebe's Search For Manhood." *Interventions,* vol. 11, no. 2, July 2009, pp. 199-202.

Kalu, Ogbu U. "Gender Ideology in Igbo Religion. The Changing Religious Role of Women in Igboland." *Africa: Rivista trimestrale di studi e documentazione dell'Istituto per l'Africa e l'Oriente*, vol. 46, no. 2, June 1991, pp. 184-202.

Liben, Lynn S. and Rebecca S. Bigler. *The Developmental Course of Gender Differentiation: Conceptualizing, Measuring, and Evaluating Constructs and Pathways.* Blackwell Publishing, 2002.

Maccoby, Eleanor E. "Gender and Group Process: A Developmental Perspective." *Current Directions in Psychological Science*, vol. 11, no. 2, Apr. 2002, pp. 54-58.

Mulvey, Kelly Lynn, and Melanie Killen. "Challenging Gender Stereotypes: Resistance and Exclusion." *Child Development*, vol. 86, no. 3, May 2015, pp. 681-694.

Onukawa, M.C. "The Chi Concept in Igbo Gender Naming." *Africa: Journal of the International African Institute*, vol. 70, no. 1, Feb. 2000, pp. 107-117.

Osei-Nyame, Kwadwo. "Chinua Achebe Writing Culture: Representations of Gender and Tradition in "Things Fall Apart"." *Research in African Literatures*, vol. 30, no. 2, Summer 1999, pp. 148-164.

Rhoads, Diana Akers. "Culture in Chinua Achebe's Things Fall Apart." *African Studies Review*, vol. 36, no. 2, Sep. 1993, pp. 61-72.

Sauntson, Helen. *Researching Language, Gender and Sexuality. A Student Guide.* Routledge, 2020.

Scheub, Harold. "'When a Man Fails Alone' A Man and His Chi in Chinua Achebe's Things Fall Apart." *Chinua Achebe's Things Fall Apart. A Casebook*, edited by Isidore Okpewho. Oxford University Press, 2003, pp. 95-122.

Stratton, Florence. *Contemporary African Literature and the Politics of Gender.* Routledge 1994.